LAVENDER

FRAGRANCE OF PROVENCE

HANS SILVESTER

TEXT BY CHRISTIANE MEUNIER

HARRY N. ABRAMS, INC.

PUBLISHERS

This book is dedicated to the country people of Provence who, by their toil, have beautified the land.

The photographs in this book were taken with Leica M6 and R6 cameras, using Kodachrome 64 and 200 film.

Translated from the French by Alexandra Campbell

First published under the title *Provence, terre de lavande* by Les Editions de La Martinière, Paris

Library of Congress Catalog Card Number: 95–78668
ISBN 0–8109–3576–7

In Provence, lavender and its hybrid lavandin are found everywhere. In winter, the fields display a strict and denuded geometry: plants are cut very short at harvest, and the branches bear only a thin greyish foliage. As soon as spring arrives, they turn a delicate green that becomes more and more intense. In June, flower buds appear on the ends of the new stalks, at first showing only a tinge of pale purple, perceptible above all when the wind blows through the fields. But the sun grows hotter and the flowers do not take long to open into a dazzling violet-blue: here comes summer! This is a period of intense activity, when workers cut the flowers and distil their essences night and day. No time is to be lost and every minute is counted. After harvest, hopes rest on the arrival of the refreshing storms of late summer, which reinvigorate the plants exhausted by flowering, heat and the operations of the cutting machines. By the end of September, all the fields are harvested. Now it is time for nature to regather its forces and, following the torrid summer, gently prepare for a winter that will, in all likelihood, be severe.

Each season offers a very different picture of the lavender and lavandin fields, but all have their own beauty, serving as symbols of the sometimes contradictory aspects of the Provençal soul, ever divided between sadness and gaiety, softness and hardness.

The fields are not all alike: those of true lavender have a somewhat 'disparate' appearance (no plant resembles its neighbour in either colour or shape); the lavandin plants, on the other hand, are very regular and extend in perfect hedges that follow the gentle curves of the land. These variations in the landscape are also a reflection of the different types of lavender farming. On the plains or plateaux, cultivation, very extensive and intensive, is mechanized and managed as a full-scale commercial enterprise, while in mountain regions, the often scattered farms are divided into small parcels that form a patchwork on the rugged, stony slopes.

In their different guises, the lavender and lavandin fields are now an established part of the landscape and activities of the South of France. It has not always been so: this cultivation came into being only at the beginning of the twentieth century.

Lavender, of course, existed in the wild long before it was farmed. It grew naturally on the sunny slopes of the hills of Provence. The plant requires a well-drained soil and a minimum altitude of about 600 metres (2,000 feet). It belongs to the Labiatae family, which comprises many other aromatic plants, including mint, thyme, oregano and sage. The vegetable tissue of these plants is distinguished by the presence of specialized cells grouped in glands which, as they mature, secrete essential aromatic oils and store them in different parts of the plant – leaves and stalks as well as flowers. The essential oil (or essence), widely used in perfumery, is extracted by distilling the flowering stalks in steam.

The secretion of essential oil (thought to be a form of adaptation by the plant to drought) is linked to the process of photosynthesis and is therefore more intense in very sunny regions. Provence thus owes its perfumes to the sun. Observation under the microscope shows that a tight felting of tiny hairs covers the surface of the plant and protects it from heat and drying out by limiting the evaporation of the water it contains.

From antiquity, there are accounts of the use of lavender to scent bath water and laundry. In the Middle Ages, with the development of medicine, and then that of perfumery, one finds regular mention of lavender and its essence. Its disinfectant powers, like its scent, were often put to use, and it was one of the plants burned in large quantities in houses and streets to fight against epidemics of plague. The illness was thought to be spread by smell, and scented fumigations were widely employed against contagion. In the archives of many Provençal towns can be found precise records of the sums spent by the community to buy vast quantities of aromatic plants, and notably lavender, from peasants, who gathered them in the hills.

Lavender essence, an efficient antiseptic, is used in Provence to treat burns and wounds in animals and people: it was long ago observed that cuts suffered while harvesting lavender with a sickle never became infected.

In parallel with such therapeutic applications, both internal and external, the use of essential lavender oils greatly increased from the Renaissance, stimulated by the local town of Grasse, which had become 'the scent capital'. Under the influence of the Italian Medici family (14th–16th centuries), who turned it into an important commercial centre, this town developed different industries exploiting the resources of the locality and its hinterland: the numerous flocks of sheep, for example, supplied both leather for the tannery and fat used in making soap and cosmetic ointments.

The fashion of the time dictated that articles made of skin should be scented – above all gloves, an essential item of dress for any person of quality of either sex – and it was the master glovers of Grasse who became the first perfumers. The scent industry at this point overtook all others, and the production of the aromatic raw materials needed for its development became an important business in Grasse and its surrounding area, and soon after in the whole region of the lower Alps.

Initially sporadic, the gathering of wild lavender on the arid hills of the French Midi became progressively more organized.

At the beginning of the nineteenth century, industrial development was to lead to depopulation on an unprecedented scale: many peasants left the country to work in factories or on the railways, then under construction. The rural exodus had important consequences for both town and country.

A symbol of luxury and social success, the use of scent had survived the upheavals of history and gradually pervaded all social classes. Rulers and nobles through the ages were avid for perfumes. Napoleon was an insatiable user of eau de Cologne and when, during his exile, he was unable to procure it, his servant created a substitute from the native plants of Saint Helena. The 'recipe' has recently been discovered in the drawer of a desk that once belonged to him. Reformulated by modern perfumers, it has enabled us to re-experience,

from the distant past, something of the olfactory atmosphere of Napoleon's exile. This anecdote is related to show how important perfume was to some of the greatest men of the time and to the upper classes in general, for whom it was a mark of distinction. It helps to explain why perfume was seen as a sign of elegance and social accomplishment, in the same way as dress.

The country people who moved to the towns were eager for such signs of refinement and did not hesitate to spend part of their earnings on luxuries either for themselves, or indeed to give to others. Fashion was no longer the preserve of a rich and idle elite; it touched all social classes.

The cosmetic and perfumery industries multiplied, particularly in France, but also in all the great cities of Europe and America. Meanwhile, the urban working population swelled greatly in number, creating a new market for manufactured goods. Consumer habits completely changed.

In the countryside, cash income was rare and people normally produced for themselves the bulk of what they personally consumed. Barter between neighbours and at market supplemented a farm's own supplies, so that a minimum of goods were, in that sense, 'bought'. Economy was the rule and money – where it existed – was allocated principally to the purchase of land to increase the property rather than to consumer goods, which were regarded as superfluous. This mentality was utterly to change with the rise of the salaried city dweller, whose income was much more readily diverted to the purchase of manufactured goods. Shops in the towns offered a wide range of wares and the working classes sought to imitate the bourgeoisie who, for their part, copied the habits of the nobility. Scent in all its manifestations had long been a feature of aristocratic life and had been used for centuries at court and by the prosperous classes. Everything was scented – gloves, doublets, wigs, handkerchiefs – indeed, it is hard now to imagine the smells that would have assailed the nostrils of our forebears, particularly as the riot of perfumes was also intended to offset questionable levels of hygiene. The demand for aromatic raw materials naturally increased in consequence; so let us now leave the

hubbub of the towns for the hills of Provence, where the poorer areas were gradually being deserted by the peasants as they forsook the land to find work in town.

These poor areas often consisted of sloping ground, at high altitude, with a shallow soil easily eroded by infrequent but very violent rains. As crops could only be produced there by incessant labour, often concentrated on small plots enclosed by little walls to shore up the earth, these arid mountain regions were the first to be abandoned. The ground showed itself highly suited to the proliferation of wild lavender, which little by little invaded the space vacated by the disenchanted peasant farmers. Lavender relishes high altitudes and stony soils that have been improved by years of patient working, and where flocks of sheep would now and then supply dung and destroy the young trees and bushes whose shade is injurious to the plant.

The abandoned hills thus became covered in wild lavender at the very moment when the perfume industry was beginning to cry out for more and more raw materials. The Grasse industry, undisputed leader in the field of scent production, was to take a particularly active interest and to set up a ring of distilleries and collection points for essences.

During the nineteenth century, wild lavender picking became increasingly organized. From being treated as a 'fringe' occupation and source of supplementary income, it became an important part of the activities of some holdings. At first it was a job for women and children, or shepherds and woodsmen in their spare time; sickle in hand, each went off to cut the wild lavender, bringing it back in a large canvas sack hung from the shoulder or, in the case of the women, in an apron. In some regions, the quantities of lavender collected were in fact measured in 'aprons'. These pickings were distilled in primitive alembics (stills) of small capacity heated by wood.

From 1850, it was the heads of the family who took charge of the matter – a sign of the new importance of the resource in the agricultural economy. Veritable 'cutting operations' were organized each summer. The teams of cutters included not only members of the family and neighbours but also outside seasonal labour – initially woodsmen and gypsies, then workers from

other countries: Italy, Spain, North Africa. At the beginning of the twentieth century, the teams consisted of up to thirty or forty people, who spent the whole week in the mountains, cutting lavender flowers with a sickle from morning to night and gathering a vast quantity each day. This could be distilled *in situ* in portable copper alembics, which were carried on the back of a donkey or mule and set up by the nearest water source.

However, in an effort to save time and energy, there was a growing tendency to increase the capacity of the apparatus, which required the building of a structure of fireproof bricks round the still and oven. This meant that it was then the cut plants that had to be transported to what were now distilleries on fixed sites. Large organizations owned their own still, but the perfume manufacturers also established a network of distilleries to encourage lavender picking and to assure their supplies of essence.

The development of wild lavender picking profoundly altered the peasants' economy and way of life at the period. Their labour, previously concentrated on farming for their own consumption, now embraced products for industrial use, creating a source of 'cash' income that enabled them, thanks to the strict economy practised in some cases through several generations, to buy more land, improve farm buildings and equipment, and to meet exceptional expenses such as social occasions, dowries, travel or family settlements.

Since lavender essence can be easily conserved for sale at a convenient moment or when the price is most favourable, the growers were enabled to 'manage' the planning of their production and to engage in forward dealing. The new resource changed behaviour and even led to serious conflict between the older generation, who believed in food production and self-sufficiency, and the younger, who were more eager to invest time and equipment in this new activity.

The distillation and sale of essences gave rise to the role of broker-distiller. This could amount to an occupation in its own right, acting for a French, or indeed foreign, perfume company. It often happened that farmers who had an alembic also distilled for their neighbours on an *ad hoc* basis. They thus became producer-distillers and often additionally acted as 'broker'; in other words, they bought the essences that they distilled and resold them to the interested manufacturers. This required a means of transport for collection and delivery of the containers of essence, and many of the brokers were, indeed, among the first car owners.

In Provence, the brokerage system also embraced other produce of industrial use, such as silk-worm cocoons, fuller's teasels (for raising the nap on cloth), wool and skins. The trade in lavender essences helped to strengthen and develop the network as well as the role of the markets and fairs at which the essences were sold, including Sault, Forcalquier and Carpentras. Farmers, brokers, industrialists and dealers regularly met there to settle their business and to fix the price. Despite the growth of modern communications, such brokerage of essences continues to this day, and fairs and markets are still used for both formal and informal business meetings.

The impact of this activity was not only immediately felt at the agricultural and business level, but also had repercussions on local artisans. Stills were generally made by independent metalworkers or boilermakers, each of whom continually sought ways to improve his apparatus. Copper was the most commonly used material, as it is easily worked with a hammer and is a good conductor of heat. It served too for the containers in which essence was transported and conserved, although these were also made from tin and later from zinc. Urban artisans thus discovered a new occupation which, from the early twentieth century, led to the establishment of small specialized industries.

Meanwhile, recognizing the value of wild lavender, landowners determined to explore all possible means to encourage its spread. They 'thinned out' the plants (removing the superfluous ones to allow the others to grow better), ploughed the land to improve the soil, and even brought manure to fertilize it. Any saplings would be grubbed up at the same time, particularly conifers, since their needles render the soil acid and harmful to other vegetation. Furthermore, as lavender loves the sun, tree cover is detrimental to it; and given the aridity of the regions concerned, any plant represents unwelcome 'rivalry' that will deplete the soil of water. Efforts were thus made to maximize the lavender's chances by eradicating the competition.

These practices did not amount to 'cultivation' in the fullest sense, however, for they were concerned with encouraging the natural spread of the wild plant rather than with establishing lavender fields. Of course, the idea of farming lavender soon followed, but early attempts did not prove very successful. These mostly took the form of uprooting young wild lavender and replanting it in the fields. However, without watering, only a relatively small proportion took root.

Cultivation on a large scale was not in fact practised until the 1920s, and then not with lavender itself but with the hybrid lavandin. Lavender (*Lavandula angustifolia*) is occasionally found at a fairly low altitude (under 500 metres or about 1,600 feet) in proximity to another plant of the same family called 'spike' (or French) lavender (*Lavandula latifolia*). Pollination between lavender and spike is naturally produced by wind or, more often, by bees which visit the flowers of both varieties in turn, carrying the pollen collected from the stamen (male organ) of one to the pistil (female organ) of the other. The seeds produced by this fertilization yield a hybrid plant, lavandin, which, with certain exceptions, is sterile.

The country people had already noted these distinctive plants, better developed and more tenacious than the rest, and christened them 'big lavender', 'great lavender' or alternatively 'bastard lavender'. The precise identification of lavandin was made by scientists whose work had a twofold purpose: to increase and control the production of essential lavender oil by cultivation of the plant; and to encourage the agricultural development of poor regions often limited by resources to the small-scale rearing of goats or sheep and a little food growing.

Various researchers applied themselves to the question, and in 1927, in the laboratories of the Société Chiris in Grasse, the artificial pollination of spike by lavender pollen led to the production of six seeds. The sowing of these seeds yielded two plants identified as 'lavandins'. Though this is commonly related as the event that marked the 'discovery' of lavandin, many other researches were conducted in parallel, resulting in a veritable 'explosion' of lavender cultivation from the 1930s.

The hybrid lavandin offers manifold advantages: a robust plant, adapting readily to difficult climatic conditions and poor soil, it grows very well, even on the open plains, and has a yield of essential oil that can be ten times that of lavender.

Efforts at cultivation were therefore directed first at lavandin. However, as with lavender, the early attempts at transplanting to a field the individual plants that occasionally occurred in the wild did not produce good results.

Lavandin being a hybrid, the pollen grains on the stamens presented anomalies that generally made the plants sterile. To bring them into cultivation, therefore, trials were made with propagation by cuttings. This involved taking little slips (cuttings) from a lavandin plant, preferably in the autumn. Carefully reared in nurseries, where they were well tended and watered, these cuttings produced roots in a few months and each one developed into a lavandin 'set' which, in the autumn or spring of the following year (eighteen months later), could be transferred to an open field.

The technique became widespread and rapidly enabled very large areas to be brought into cultivation, not only small plots in mountainous regions, but also fields of several hectares in less rugged parts: the valleys of the Asse, the Valensole plateau (Alpes-de-Haute-Provence), Baronnies (Drôme), and eventually in the valleys of the Rhône, the Gard and the Ardèche.

Initially, the cuttings were taken from wild lavandin plants found growing naturally. This produced the first variety of lavandin, called 'Ordinary'. In the 1930s, another more productive variety was developed by Professor Abrial. It bears his name, 'Abrial' (or 'Abrialis') lavandin, which up to the 1960s accounted for more than two-thirds of the planted area.

During this period lavandin cultivation was afflicted by a 'wasting' ailment that caused the plants to yellow and rapidly die. The life-span of the fields shrank from 8–10 years to 3–4 years. As there was no known remedy, efforts were made to find more resistant varieties, and the most successful were adopted. These were the 'Super' lavandins of the 1950s and 1960s, followed by 'Grosso', the dominant variety from 1975. Grosso lavandin now accounts for more than three-quarters of the cultivated area, the remainder being divided equally between Abrial, Super and a variety closely related to Abrial called 'Sumian'.

Meanwhile, the gathering of wild lavender continued up to the 1950s, in parallel with its developing cultivation. The lavender was grown from seed, being, unlike lavandin, a fertile plant.

The mastery of lavender, and above all lavandin, cultivation led to the planting of extensive areas of land. Industrial demand for essential lavandin oil – cheaper than that of lavender and well suited to soap-making in particular – continued to increase. In 1923 in Provence 100 tons of lavender essence were produced, 90% of which was obtained from wild lavender. The cultivated variety accounted for the remaining 10%. By about 1950, the picking of wild lavender had virtually been abandoned. Overall production of lavender essence had declined to 80 tons, with the relative proportions of the wild and the cultivated plant reversed: only 10% of the tonnage of essence now came from pickings of the wild plant; the other 90% was of cultivated origin. Today, production of lavender essence in Provence has reduced to some 25 tons per year. The plant is more difficult to grow and its cultivation, necessarily at a high altitude, lends itself less readily to mechanization than lavandin. Its use in perfumery has declined in the face of competition from less expensive products and of changes of fashion.

In the case of the hybrid lavandin, in 1924 cultivation in Provence produced 1 or 2 tons of essential oil. By 1950 this figure had risen to 200 tons; then, stimulated by economic growth and the huge increase in the use of detergents, production between 1960 and 1980 rose from 500 to 1,000 tons. Currently the annual production of lavandin essence is in excess of 1,000 tons, principally used to scent detergents. Lavandin essence is well suited to mass consumption: its price remains competitive by comparison with rival natural products as well as synthetic alternatives, the emergence of the chemical industry after the Second World War having led to an influx of new scented products on the market, notably derived from petrochemicals. These chemical products are able to imitate natural fragrances or create wholly original ones, and they have rapidly claimed the lion's share of the action in every field of perfumery. Some natural products have, nevertheless, successfully endured, among them lavandin, which is still widely used as a raw material because it represents good value for money.

The increase in yield and decrease in costs of lavandin production have been achieved by dedicated and concerted efforts at improving the quality of the plants as well as the methods and techniques of cultivation, harvesting and distillation.

Quality
This is measured by several criteria:
Volume of vegetable mass. The greater the volume, the greater the yield of flowers per hectare.

Vigour and longevity. The longer the field lasts (about eight years) the sooner the prime cost of cultivation is amortized.

Suitability for mechanized cultivation. A plant with long stalks and deep roots lends itself better, for example, to harvesting by machine.

Yield of essential oil. Essential oils are valued by their olfactory and analytic characteristics, measured against precise norms that reflect the needs of the industries using them.

In the attempt to unite all these qualities in a single plant, producers took cuttings from specimens that appeared remarkable in volume, vigour and yield. This method made it possible to obtain from one set (the 'clone ancestor') a series of individual plants that were all identical, constituting a 'clone'. The research done in this area over the past twenty years has now achieved practical results, giving a producer laying down a field the choice of two types of set.

One is obtained by the traditional method, in which cuttings are taken from a plant known as a 'stool' and grown into sets in nurseries. This method is the more economical, since it requires no special material; on the other hand, the varietal purity of the stool is not guaranteed and neither is the health of the set, which may carry parasites or disease, inherited from the stool or acquired in the environment in which it was reared.

The alternative type is now available from specialist nurseries: instead of a woody cutting, the ends of young leafy shoots – 'herbaceous cuttings' – are taken from the stool and grown under glass in small pots below ground, kept moist and supplied with all the elements they need to grow. The sets are ready to be planted out in about two months, rather than twelve or eighteen months by the traditional method. These sets are more expensive but, grown in a protected environment, they are free of pathogenic germs and the fields have a longer life-span. The initial investment in establishing the field can thus be amortized over a greater number of harvests.

Further to improve the health status and varietal purity of the sets, cells taken from the bud of a lavandin shoot have been developed in the laboratory ('*in vitro*'). These cells are grown in a suitable nutrient in a test-tube, where they multiply to form a plantlet that is in its turn divided in the laboratory. The plantlets are then transplanted to small pots and acclimatized under glass. The resulting plants thus present a perfect genetic identity.

The same reproduction techniques can be applied to other plants, including true lavender. Side by side with the lavender traditionally obtained by seed ('fine lavender'), there also exist lavenders propagated by cuttings; these are called 'clonal lavenders'.

The fields of fine lavender are very heterogeneous in appearance because each plant comes from a seed that carries its own genetic code, with the colour, form, volume and quality of essential oil varying from individual to individual. This is known as a 'population' of different individuals. In contrast, the fields of clonal lavender, like those of lavandin, display rows of identical plants because they all come from the same clone.

The clonal lavenders have a better yield than the fine lavender, and their cultivation, which is easier, can be virtually identical to that of lavandin. Their essential oils are thus less expensive and more saleable. For these various reasons, the cultivation of clonal lavender has developed more and more, while the fine lavender is confined to small plots at a high altitude.

Planting

This takes place in autumn, or spring if the climate carries the threat of a severe winter. In high altitudes or regions exposed to the blowing of the mistral, repeated frosts can be damaging to the young plants.

From the very beginning of lavender and lavandin cultivation (1920–30), the plants have been set out in lines, with enough space between the rows and between the individual plants in a row to allow them to be easily tended and to be cut with a sickle.

When cutting machines came into use around 1950, the spacing of the plants was calculated in accordance with the type of cutter used. Mechanization was slow in becoming established, however, since the fields had a life-span of some years and it was necessary to wait until they needed to be replanted. Only from the 1960s did harvesting by machine become truly widespread; and twenty years later, harvesting by hand had virtually ceased to exist.

For a field to be suitable for machine cutting, the plants must be set very closely in line and present a continuous, dense and uniform vegetable mass. Deep, spreading roots are essential if every plant is to draw an adequate supply of water from the soil and to withstand the annual assault of the cutting machine.

The sets obtained from herbaceous cuttings have a regularly developed root system that perfectly meets these requirements. Moreover, they are all of fairly comparable size and shape, which also facilitates mechanized planting. The planting machines have not been specifically designed for the purpose, but have been adapted from those used to plant tobacco or potatoes, for example.

About 10,000 sets of lavandin are planted per hectare, and 15,000 of lavender. Planting by hand is now increasingly limited to small areas and to replacement of the few sets that do not take or that die in the first years of growth.

Agricultural management

Ideally, watering should be done at the time of planting and after each harvest, when the plants are particularly in need of replenishment, although they are able to survive long periods of drought. Some planting machines have devices that supply a little water to each set as it is put into the ground, helping it to take root.

The field needs to be cleaned once or twice a year, either with herbicides or mechanically, since weeds not only take some of the water from the soil – already in short supply – but can obstruct the cutting blades and the movement of the machines. Moreover, some weeds, if harvested and distilled with lavender or lavandin, impart unwanted scents or colours to the essences. Most fields are thus carefully tended and kept completely free of weeds.

In areas of long-established intensive production, such as the Valensole plateau, lavandin has, ever since 1935, been virtually the sole crop. The soil has progressively become so depleted that, after twenty or thirty years of successive, uninterrupted plantings, the lavandin became afflicted by parasites and various diseases, significantly reducing its life-span and yield of essential oil.

To combat this 'wasting', curative and preventive treatments have been developed; but, above all, ways of 'reconstituting' the soil have had to be found. Many of the lavender and lavandin fields have thus been replaced by crops of durum wheat, soya or sunflowers. In summer, their dazzling yellows are juxtaposed to the deep violet-blue of the lavandin, presenting a wonderful contrast of colours. These crops are often cultivated in rotation with lavandin. Others used for the same purpose are forage crops (clover, sainfoin) and 'green fertilizers' (vetch), which are not harvested but are ploughed into the earth to regenerate it.

Harvesting

Harvesting is generally done from mid-July to mid-August, depending on the maturity of the plants, which differs, among other things, according to their variety and to the climatic conditions. The best yields of essential oil are obtained when 80% of the flowers are in full bloom, or even slightly withered.

Although cutting machines were first invented in 1925, it was only in the 1960s that mechanized cutting become fully established. To begin with, only the large lavandin fields on level ground could be harvested by machine. Gradually, both machines and plants have been adapted and now even fine lavender is mechanically gathered.

Harvesting a hectare (about 2 ½ acres) with a sickle used to take two fast workers two or three days. The same job by machine takes two men two or three hours. This is an average based on the classic cutting machines that cut one row at a time. However, over very extensive areas (such as the Valensole plateau) machines that cut three rows at a time are in use. The cutting machines bind the plants in sheaves. These are then left in the field for two or three days to lose their surplus moisture before they are taken to the distillery.

Distillation

Steam distillation is thought to have been invented, or at any rate perfected, by the Arabs. The method involves passing a jet of steam through the matter to be distilled. The steam frees and carries with it the volatile essential oil contained in the plant's secretory glands. The mixture of steam and essential oil is then cooled. It condenses and returns to a liquid state. It is collected in a Florentine flask called a 'separator' fitted with two taps at different levels. In the separator, by decantation, the essential oil naturally separates from the water; being lighter, it floats to the surface and can then be drawn off through the upper tap.

The small copper stills of 200–500 litre (45–110 gallon) capacity commonly in use at the beginning of the century were quickly replaced by much larger installations, starting in the regions where production was highest. There are now several hundred distilleries of various sizes in Provence. They belong to private distillers, businesses or producers' cooperatives. The cost of distillation is paid by the producer per kilo of essence obtained; this represents a significant proportion (15–20%) of the selling price, which explains the constant concern to improve the techniques and apparatus employed.

In general, a distillery comprises at least two stills (or alembics) of 5,000 or 6,000 litres (1,100–1,300 gallons) each. A still contains 800 to 1,000 kilos (almost a ton) of plants, customarily compressed with a tractor tyre filled with concrete, so as to pack in as much as possible. Water is not put inside the still, as used to be the custom; now the steam is produced outside, enters through the bottom of the still, and then forces itself through the plant mass, where it becomes laden with essential oil. The resulting mixture of oil vapour and steam flows over through the 'swan-neck' to the condensor coil (or 'worm'). This is a coiled tube immersed in circulating cold water. Thus, the mixture of vapours condenses to water and essential oil.

It takes about thirty minutes to complete the distillation process. The volume of water used in cooling is more or less equal to that of the still, in this case 5,000–6,000 litres (1,100–1,300 gallons). This explains the customary siting of distilleries near a watercourse.

Traditionally, the heat needed to produce the steam was provided by burning previously distilled lavender stalks. However, some distilleries now use electric, gas or oil-fired boilers. The yields of essential oil are less than 1% for fine lavender and 2–3% for lavandin, depending on the variety. This means that 120–130 kg (or lbs) of lavender flowers must be distilled to obtain 1 kg (or lb) of essence, whereas with lavandin between 35 and 70 kg (or lbs) would suffice. Also, because of lavender's lighter vegetable mass, while a hectare of lavender gives on average 15–20 kg of essence (13–18 lbs per acre), a hectare of lavandin produces roughly 100 kg (90 lbs per acre), with top yields in excess of 200 kg (180 lbs per acre).

A number of years ago, a new technique began to be adopted imitating that used in the United States to distil mint. A huge container with a capacity of 10–15 cubic metres (350–530 cubic feet) is transported to the fields on a truck. A machine called a 'silo filler' harvests the plants and chops them into small pieces that are then tipped into the container. When full, the container is next taken to the distillery and covered with a lid equipped with an outlet to a cooling system. The container itself, fitted with a steam inlet, becomes the still. Once distillation is finished, the tubes are removed and the container is taken to a field where the distillation residues are tipped out, usually serving as fertilizer. In the last few years, this new system has proved highly successful, as it allows large quantities to be quickly processed with limited manpower, there being no loading or unloading costs. Several distilleries have already been designed to accommodate this method, and it is estimated that in 1994 some 15% of the lavandin harvest in Provence was thus distilled, 'in container'.

Commercialization

The essential oils are sold through the agency of brokers, dealers or groups of producers. Few producers sell directly to the consumer, although this occasionally happens, particularly with lavender essences intended for pharmaceutical use, aromatherapy or luxury perfumery. Here, however, the quantities involved are limited, rarely amounting to more than 200 kg (440 lbs), and price is not the determining factor.

Lavender and lavandin are never used in the pure state, but are combined with other natural or synthetic materials to make a 'compound' that will add fragrance to a given vehicle. This may, for example, be an alcoholic solution (for an eau de toilette) or a detergent base (soaps and washing powders).

To create a compound, the perfumer has recourse to hundreds of raw materials. He chooses and combines them rather as a musician composes with sounds, bearing in mind the product that the compound will ultimately scent. Even if his formula includes lavender or lavandin, the compound will not necessarily be dominated by either, which explains why the lavenders and lavandins sometimes pass 'unnoticed' by the eye – or rather nose – of consumers.

The price of the compound should, of course, reflect that of the end product for which it is intended. Some large perfumery or soap companies have their own laboratories for the formulation and fabrication of compounds. But many turn to specialized businesses that offer a full range of compounds in all kinds of vehicles and are also equipped to create others to order.

Most of the lavender and lavandin essences produced in the South of France are sold for export. The leading market is the United States, followed by Germany, England and Switzerland. Other European countries are also important consumers, as are Latin America and Japan. In fact, all countries are consumers, either directly, when engaged in industries that use the raw materials, or indirectly, when buying the perfumed compounds or finished products that contain them. The main clients are multinational companies looking, above all, for regular supplies of reliable quality at the best prices.

The lavender and lavandin essences of Provence are thus in constant competition with other natural raw materials or synthetic alternatives being produced throughout the world. The pressure of international competition is extremely strong and the need to adapt to the industrial market requires continual effort by the growers. In regions where the geography allows, mechanization has been developed to the maximum and everything concerned with distilling is carefully maintained and thoroughly up-to-date. There is thus a concentration of lavandin growing in the départements of Alpes-de-Haute-Provence, Drôme and Vaucluse – areas with little irregularity of relief, where cultivation is possible over wide expanses.

The total area of lavandin cultivation in Provence is estimated at roughly 14,000 hectares (54 square miles) divided between 2,000 producers. Half of this lies on the Valensole and Albion plateaux, and a quarter on other regions of flat open country, as in the Vallée du Rhône. In the regions of Valensole-Puimichel, Sault and Banon, nearly half of the growers cultivate more than 20 hectares (50 acres) each. In contrast, in the Vallée du Rhône, round Apt and Diois-Baronnies (Drôme),

the average area devoted to the lavandin crop is 5–7 hectares (12–17 acres) per farm.

The cultivation of true lavender has gradually been abandoned in the highest and most rugged regions (Hautes-Alpes) and in those somewhat isolated from the large production areas. Lavender farming involves roughly 3,000 hectares (12 square miles). But fine lavender (obtained from seeds) has declined in favour of clonal lavender (propagated by cuttings) and these crops tend to be concentrated in the same regions as lavandin: Drôme, Vaucluse, Alpes-de-Haute-Provence.*

For all the regions concerned, lavender/lavandin cultivation represents an important, if not the most important, agricultural option. It is part of a fragile balance of economic activity, often very long-established: beekeeping, for example, is traditionally associated with lavender/lavandin plants, which are exceptionally rich in nectar. In feeding on this, bees stop the plant secreting, and the quantity of sugar thus 'economized' by the flowers improves the yield of essential oil. Moreover, the bee is a highly efficient means of pollination for those lavender species that are fertile. This 'exchange of good practices' has long been observed, and the seasonal moving of the hives is arranged to coincide with the flowering periods of the different areas of lavender cultivation.

Other aromatic and scented plants are cultivated in Provence for distillation (clary, hyssop, tarragon) or for drying or freezing (thyme, basil, rosemary). The gathering of wild plants has been largely overtaken by extensive cultivation, but nonetheless persists in response to demand, particularly from pharmaceutical herbalists. The picking of lime blossom, for instance, remains important in the Baronnies region. It is in effect semi-cultivated. The flowers are sold for tea (*tilleul*) and the lime-blossom markets in early July are especially picturesque.

Among the resources no longer wholly wild but not truly cultivated, the truffle holds pride of place. It grows naturally at the foot of particular oak trees. Not knowing how to cultivate the delicacy, people plant the oaks associated with them, in the hope that, with a bit of luck, the truffles will follow. This is why one often sees, between the rows of lavandin, lines of young trees intended as future truffle oaks. While waiting for them to grow, there is time for a few lavandin harvests, and also time to train a dog or a pig to search for the truffles that the oaks will surely attract.

On the plains, and varying from region to region, agriculture offers a greater range of possibilities, from fruit trees to cereals to vines; but in the mountains, a few almond trees, a flock of sheep or goats, game shooting and mushroom gathering in autumn are often the only complements to the main source of revenue: the lavender or lavandin. To ensure that the inhabitants remain, it is vital that this crop should continue to be cultivated.

The presence of a permanent and thriving rural population is essential to the continuance and proper usage of the Provençal countryside. The lavender and lavandin fields are now so much a part of the landscape that it is easy to forget that they are in no way 'natural'. They are the result of continuous and exacting labour that has given to an often very unrewarding region all the charm of a garden. In this sense, the lavender and lavandin crop is part of the 'aesthetic heritage' of Provence and should be preserved as much for this reason as for its economic importance.

All statistical data come from the Annual Report 1993 of the Office National Interprofessionnel des Plantes à Parfums, Aromatiques et Médicinales at Volx (Alpes-de-Haute-Provence).

THE LAVENDER
FIELDS

50

70

106

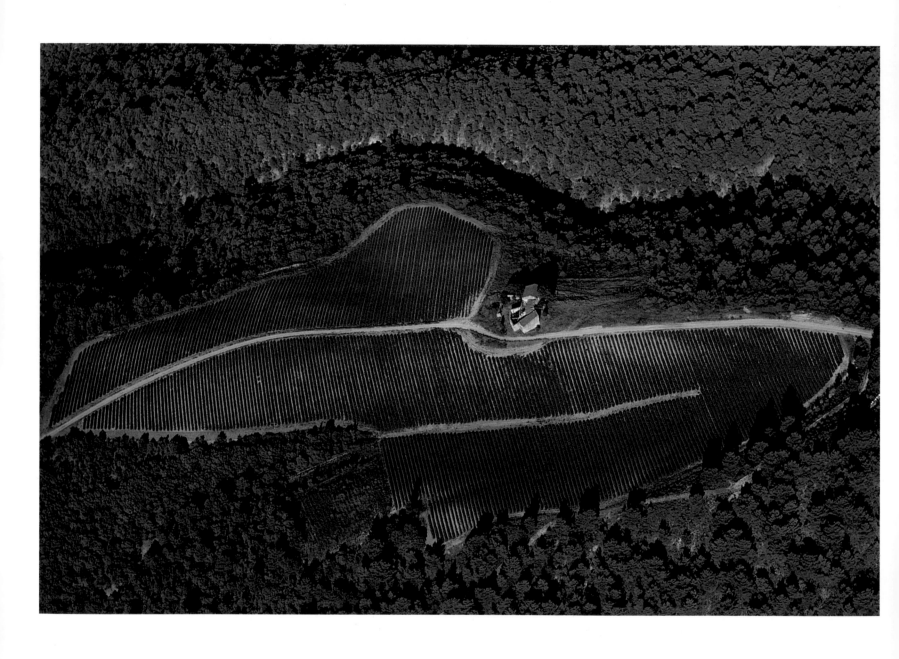

140

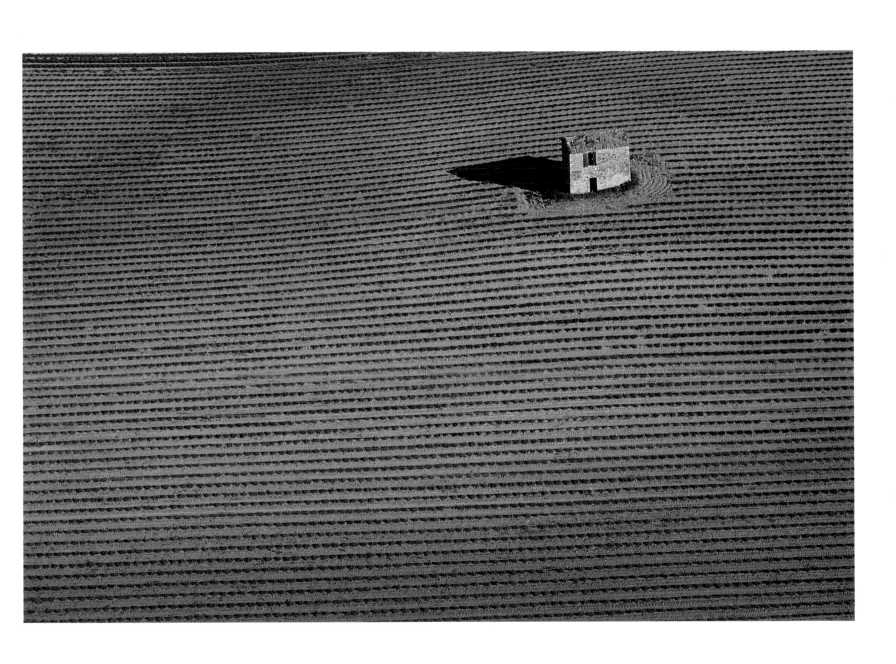

142

144

148

156